Twelve Days of Bethlehem

A Christmas Activity Book for Families

Michael & Pamela Collier

ISBN: 9781729288368

Published by Collier Creations and available for on-line purchase from Amazon

Details of other books by these authors are available on the series website:

http://colliercreations.weebly.com

The authors may be contacted by e-mail as follows:
collier1942@yahoo.co.uk
pamcollier1943@yahoo.co.uk

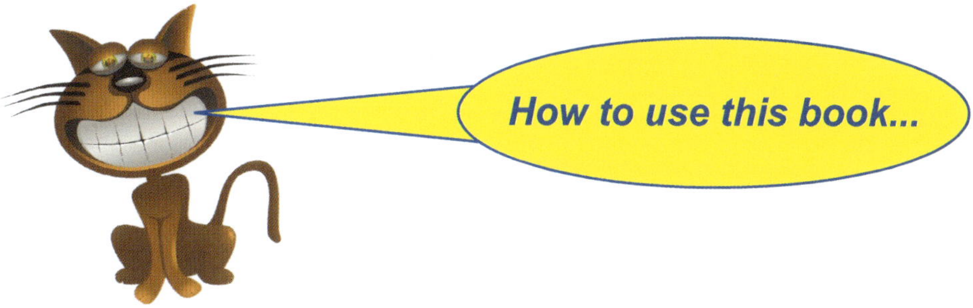

The idea is that you might like to take some family time for twelve days around Christmas to relive the ancient story of what happened in Israel long ago.

Each day tells a small part of the whole story - with forty puzzles, riddles, jokes and other activities for your whole family to do whenever you like.

You can sit at the breakfast table, cuddle round the fire or gather in an igloo in the garden (take your hot water bottle). There are things for all ages from four years to grandads.

The answers to all the puzzles and riddles can be found on the website http://colliercreations.weebly.com.

Have a great Christmas with your family!

Contents

First Day

Strange Visitor

It came as quite a shock! After washing up the breakfast in her family's house in Nazareth, she was expecting to go to the market for a nice chat with her other young friends. Of course, she would do some shopping as well.

Covering her head with a cloth, as all unmarried girls must do, she picked up a basket and headed for the door.

Help! There was a man standing inside the door! And it wasn't her fiance Joseph. He didn't really look like an ordinary man.

"Sorry to frighten you, Mary," he whispered to her. "I'll do you no harm."

"Who are you?" she stammered.

"A messenger from God – if you can believe it."

"Is this a dream, or some kind of game?"

"Certainly not – God wants you to know that he thinks highly of you. In fact, you'll have a child sent by God."

"But I'm not even married!"

"Leave God to look after that!"

Try this puzzle!
All these words are found in the story above. See if you can unscramble them.

1. OPJESH ____________________
2. MYAR ____________________
3. AZHETRNA ____________________
4. EGENRSSEM ____________________
5. MRADIER ____________________
6. RTAMKE ____________________
7. REAMD ____________________
8. GDO ____________________
9. STBAEK ____________________
10. BRFAKSATE ____________________

Some Christmas Riddles

1. In which years are Christmas & New Year in the same year?
2. Which Christmas carol is the favourite of parents?
3. Who is never hungry at Christmas?

Why do we have Christmas trees?

For centuries people have celebrated the mid-point of the winter season, and in northern Europe they often put a fir tree in the house. Its evergreen nature suggested that spring was coming, and later on Christians saw the idea of everlasting life in it.

The practice of decorating the tree became very popular when Queen Victoria and Prince Albert started to hang bright, shiny ornaments on their Christmas trees in the 1800s.

Following World War II, Norway was grateful for the help that Britain had given, and decided to give a tall fir tree to be erected in London every December.

Here is your first secret code!

Each letter has been given a number. All you have to do is look up the numbers to find the original message.

A	B	C	D	E	F	G	H	I	J	K	L	M
65	66	67	68	69	70	71	72	73	74	75	76	77
N	O	P	Q	R	S	T	U	V	W	X	Y	Z
78	79	80	81	82	83	84	85	86	87	88	89	90

Now try to decode the sentence below...

67 72 82 73 83 84 77 65 83 67 79 77 69 83
66 85 84 79 78 67 69 65 89 69 65 82.

Across
2. France
5. USA
8. Italy
9. Zimbabwe
10. Japan

Down
1. Chile
3. Australia
4. UK
6. Botswana
7. Ecuador

Know your Capital Cities

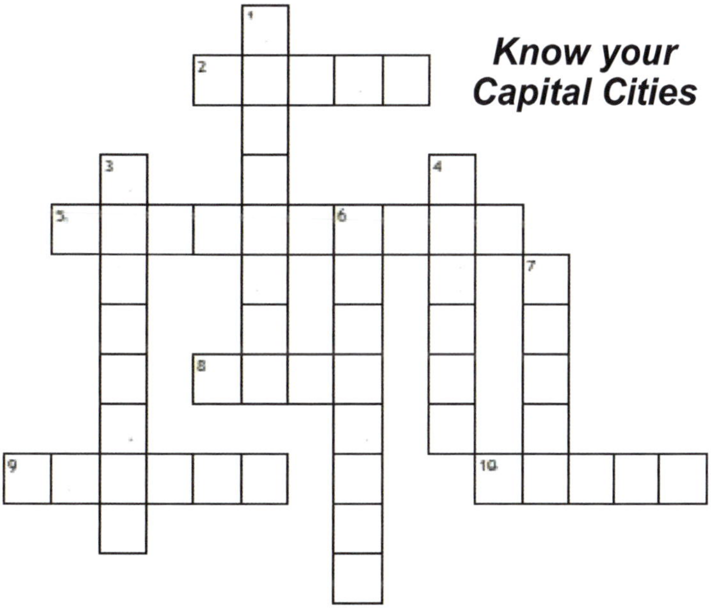

Second Day

Doubtful Dad

Covered in sweat and sawdust, Joseph the local carpenter was daydreaming while sanding the spokes for a new wheel. His mind was on the delightful girl who would soon be his wife.

There was a bang at the door – his good friend Jacob burst in.

"Hi Jake, are you all right - you look done in?" asked Joseph.

"I'm okay, but there are some terrible rumours in the street."

"About what?"

"Sorry to say... your sweet Mary has played you false."

"Whatever are you talking about?"

"It's now clear that she is pregnant – and whether it's your baby or not, you two are not married."

"What nonsense is this?" Joseph thundered angrily. "It's certainly not my child."

Joseph sank down onto the dusty floor, put his head in his hands and cried. His friend slipped out of the door.

As he became calmer, he decided what to do. "I'll just quietly break the agreement – and we'll have to go our own ways."

Hearing a sound behind him, he uttered, "Still here, Jacob?"

"No, I bring you a message from God," whispered a voice.

Turning to look, Joseph saw a strange young man by the door.

"Joseph, listen! God's got his hand in all this. Mary has been true to you – the child has been put there by God. Trust him."

Spot the ten differences in the carpenter's workshop

Check-Mate in One

You are white, and are playing from the nearer end of the board.

It's your move. Can you check-mate in one move?

Find the Odd One Out!!

!

1. February, December, March, Monday, April, June, January

2. 

3. Grape, Cauliflower, Lettuce, Asparagus, Cucumber, Potato

4. 

5. London, New York, Dehli, Paris, Beijing, Tokyo, Sydney, Madrid

6. 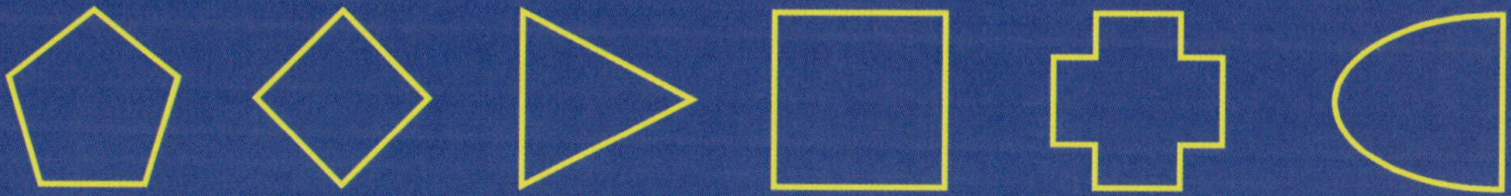

7. Denly, Root, Ali, Kane, Woakes, Curran, Stokes

Try this Sudoku

All you have to do is put numbers in the blank spaces, so that no numbers appear twice in the same row, same column or same 3x3 square region.

This is an easy one - there's a harder one later on!

6	2	1	3		5		8	9
4	5	7	2	9	8		6	3
	8		7	1	6	2	5	4
2	6		1	3	4			8
	7		6		9			1
1	9	4	5	8	7	3	2	6
7		6	9					2
	3	2	4	7	1	6	9	5
	1	9	8	6	2	4	3	7

The answers to all the puzzles are at: www.colliercreations.weebly.com

Huge Hike

Third Day

Eighty long miles – with no taxis or bikes! Joseph and Mary, who were engaged, began the worst journey of their lives.

Mary, in an advanced state of pregnancy, was being bounced about on the back of an unhappy donkey. Joseph walked all the way, leading the uncooperative beast.

The reason for all this was that the government wanted more taxes from the people.

"Everyone is ordered to their family home to register with the inland revenue department," was the instruction that had been relayed across the land.

Not that it was even their own government – because Israel in those days was an occupied country invaded by the Roman armies. The taxes were wanted by the greedy emperor of Rome, Caesar Augustus, to win more battles.

Although Nazareth was in the north of Israel, Joseph's family came from Bethlehem far to the south. Hence the long journey at such short notice.

Happily Mary managed the long trek without the baby being born onto the back of the donkey – and at last they reached Bethlehem.

Both were weary, hungry and dispirited - and the donkey too.

Which route did they take?

Look at this map of Israel and see which of the white roads would have taken Joseph and Mary all the way from Nazareth to Bethlehem.

In fact this is probably the route they used.

Junior Sudoku

Find numbers (between 1 and 4) to fill all the empty spaces, so that no number appears twice in any row, column or square section.

1			2
		3	
	2	1	4

Here is a picture for you to colour

Who am I ?

The legend of Santa Claus can be traced back hundreds of years to a monk named St. Nicholas. It is believed that he was born sometime around 280 A.D. in Patara in modern-day Turkey. Much admired for his faith and kindness, he became the subject of many legends.

He gave away all his inherited wealth and travelled the countryside helping the poor and sick. One time he saved three poor sisters from being sold into slavery or prostitution by providing them with dowries so that they could be married.

Santa Claus comes from a dialect of Dutch as "Sante Klaas" meaning St. Nicholas.

The answers to all the puzzles are at: www.colliercreations.weebly.com

No Late Rooms

Fourth Day

Of course Joseph had relatives living in Bethlehem, some of whom he had not seen for a long time - and some never at all. Since there were no telephones, the young couple just pitched up without any warning.

They were warmly welcomed, but with all the extended family converging on the little town, there was a real problem of accommodation. Everyone who had any connection with the area was there, and frantically striving for a place to stay.

Bethlehem was home to only about 300 people at that time, and the new government regulations had swollen the town's population to many times its normal size.

After a struggle, the young couple managed to squeeze in somewhere, although it wasn't very comfy. But only just in time! Mary felt that the birth of their child would happen very soon. They unpacked their goods and fed the grumpy donkey.

Joseph made up a simple bed for the new mother, and they sat down to see what would happen.

P	E	S	T	R	U	G	G	L	E	P	H	G	T
O	X	E	N	E	D	L	I	H	C	A	H	E	X
P	I	M	R	X	I	E	I	P	N	L	L	U	T
U	D	U	E	T	O	E	O	D	U	E	M	N	N
L	Y	T	L	E	U	L	P	Y	P	D	U	P	E
A	T	Y	A	N	Y	G	R	H	R	N	I	A	M
T	U	E	T	D	R	A	O	P	O	S	Y	C	N
I	T	K	I	E	M	N	N	U	G	A	S	K	R
O	E	N	V	D	E	P	E	L	T	O	U	E	E
N	E	O	E	S	A	Y	P	M	U	R	G	D	V
E	T	D	S	N	V	E	Y	O	Y	P	E	L	O
M	E	H	E	L	H	T	E	B	T	S	Z	N	G
E	E	D	X	P	S	S	Q	U	E	E	Z	E	S
C	E	P	L	S	E	M	A	R	E	C	A	R	B

Try this Wordsearch which contains twelve words from the story today.

Who was this Wenceslas fellow?

"Good King Wenceslas" is a rather strange carol that does not even mention Christmas. It tells about a king who went on a journey in harsh winter weather to give aid to a poor peasant on the Feast of Stephen (now called Boxing Day).

The English hymnwriter John Mason Neale wrote the lyrics in 1853, based on legends about Vaclav, Duke of Bohemia in AD 907–935. Apparently he was a wise and generous ruler, known by his people as Vaclav the Good.

Unfortunately not everyone agreed - and he was assassinated by his wicked brother Boleslaw the Bad. Not a happy ending!

Today he is regarded as the patron saint of the Czech Republic, and the main square in Prague is named after him.

The Pig-pen Code

Each letter is represented by the lines near it in the diagrams below. If there is a dot, then it is shown in the code symbol.

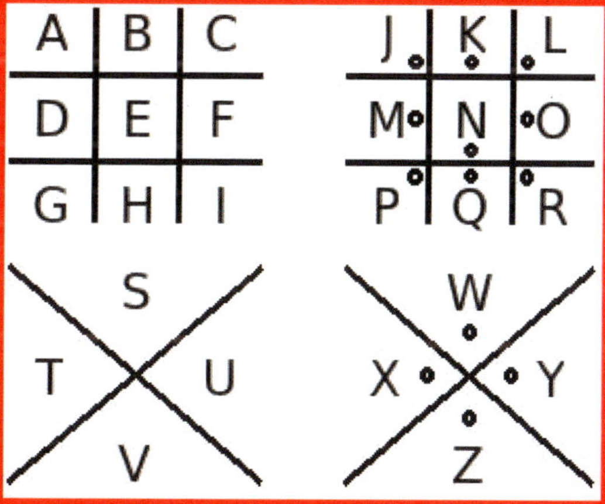

For example,  ***means "R".***

Now try to work out the following message...

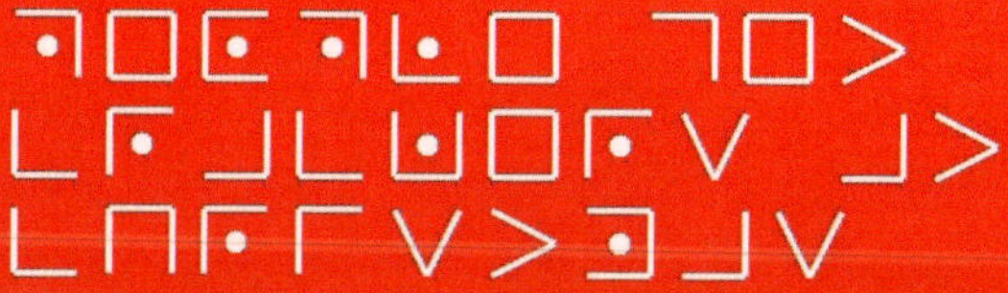

Some more Christmas riddles

What do you get if you cross a duck with some mistletoe?

What do you have in December that you don't have in any other month?

What did Mrs. Claus say to Santa when she looked at the stormy sky?

Remember that the answers to all the puzzles and riddles are at: www.colliercreations.weebly.com

Fifth Day

Major Miracle

Within a few days the new arrival popped into the family. Just like every other baby, he announced his presence with a loud cry as he exercised his little lungs. His parents were overwhelmed with the gift of their son.

Everyone was very kind and were pleased to lend Mary clothes for the infant. But Mary really wished she were back in Nazareth where she had already made preparations for the birth.

“There’s no nice crib for our child,” she complained petulantly.

“Don’t worry, love,” Joseph answered gently. “I’ve cleaned out one of the feeding troughs where the animals are fed. It’s not perfect – but quite serviceable.”

“I’m sure the baby won’t notice,” replied Mary more happily.

Regarding a name for the newborn, there was no problem. They had been told by God's messengers that they should call him ‘Yeshua’, which in modern English is ‘Jesus’. It means “the one who rescues”. Later on, many folk realised that he lived up to his name by rescuing mankind from the mess that they had made of the world.

After a few nights the many visitors to Bethlehem finished their registration and began to return home. Mary was in no state of health to make the long journey to the north of the country, and so Joseph looked for better accommodation than the cramped quarters they had accepted at first. Eventually he managed to find a suitable lodging place for the rest of their stay.

Octagon Search

For each of the coloured shapes, see how many words (3 letters or more) you can make from today's story, using some or all of the letters. But each word must use the letter in the middle. Letters can be used twice in a word.

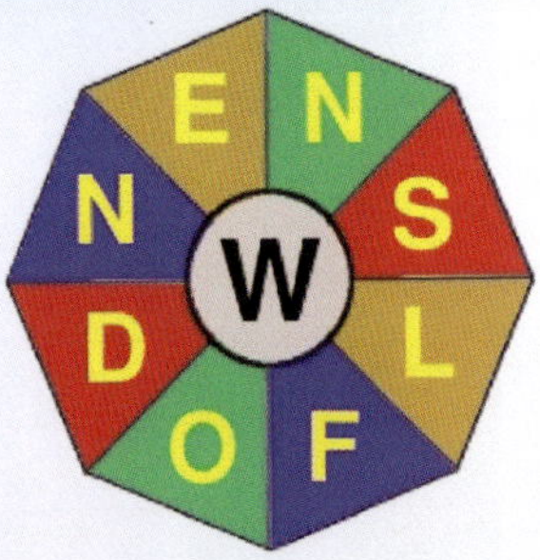

What is Christmas about?

Party poppers, Christmas crackers, mistletoe and lights.
Lots of fun and parties long, that run into the nights.
That's what Christmas is about, a lot of people say.
It's food and drink and good TV we watch on Christmas Day.

Christmas Cards, lights in town, and shops all bright and warm.
Helping old folks down the street - all lonely and forlorn.
That's what Christmas is about, a lot of people say.
Families and lots of fun we have on Christmas Day.

Christmas cards so kindly meant with Santa's presents too.
Fairy grottos for the kids, and greetings now to you.
That's what Christmas is about, a lot of people say.
We only talk to Aunty Joan because it's Christmas Day.

I wonder what you'd think of me if I said it wasn't true.
That these are things we've added on, the truth I'm telling you.
I know what Christmas is about a lot of people say -
It's Happy Birthday, Jesus - because it's God's Great Day.

Know your Famous People

Across

4. Black SA president
5. Sailing the world alone
6. PM in WW2

Down

1. Four minute mile
2. Everest first
3. Hogwarts

Sixth Day

Woolly Watchers

Meanwhile some really odd things were happening that same night on the hillsides outside Bethlehem. Many of the people in the town were shepherds, and they took it in turns to do night duty among the flocks.

Suddenly the sky was alive with brightly-lit figures, and the superstitious fellows collapsed on the ground.

"What's going on here?" one cried tremulously.

"Don't be frightened!" said a voice from the sky – which made them even more frightened.

"I've got good news for you. There is a new baby, and he's going to rescue your country from it's troubles. And you too."

"Let's go and have a look!" exclaimed one shepherd boldly.

"But what about the sheep?"

"Oh, we'll take the lambs. As for the sheep, God will look after them."

So they trooped down to the town, and soon found the place and the child. Sensing that this was a special moment from God, they crept into the room and bowed before the new rescuer.

Where's Woolly?

Among all these sheep it seems that one ram has crept in (the one with horns). Can you find him?

How many sheep are there including the ram?

A man built a house which was square, with windows on all four walls. Every window looked southward.
A bear walked past the house.
What colour was the bear?

Save the Sheep!

One of the lambs has strayed away from the shepherds. Find your way through the maze to reach him.

Can you believe your eyes?

Look carefully at this picture of a chess board, and you will see that a pair of squares are marked A and B.

What is the difference in colour between A and B?

Surprisingly, they are the same colour! Can you prove it to yourself and then to your friends?
See Tenth Day if you are still puzzled.

Seventh Day

Starry Gazers

Far away in the land that we now call Iraq, some astronomers noticed an unusual arrangement of the stars and planets in the night sky. This had never happened before, and so they pored through books which explained the meanings of such things.
"I've found it!" shouted one of them. "When you see that pattern in the sky, it signifies that a king is about to be born."
"But where in the world will that be?"
"That particular constellation always refers to Israel."
"Oh, that's a long way off. But I'm keen to see this wonder."
"Okay, boys, to horse! - well, I mean, to camel."
Weeks later a group of dusty travellers arrived in the capital city of Israel. They rode to the main palace in Jerusalem, and asked to see the newborn king. The current monarch, a slimy fellow called Herod, was rather put out to hear of a competitor being born. His advisors said the there were some prophecies concerning the village of Bethlehem and a promised king.
So the foreign visitors left the palace and headed to nearby Bethlehem, where they found the child. The astronomers had brought expensive gifts which were laid before the baby.

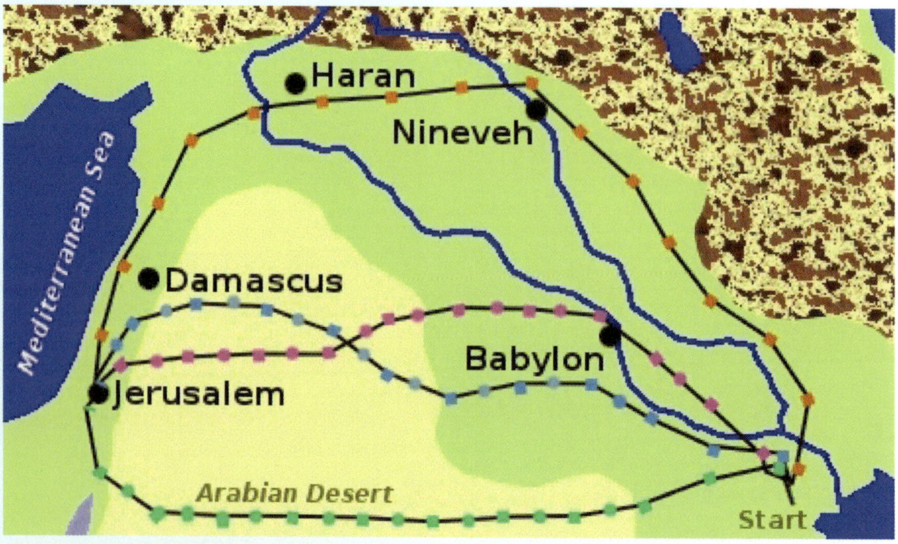

Which is the quickest route from Start to Jerusalem?

The map shows several possible routes, where each coloured square is a one-night stop. Which route would have brought them to their destination in the shortest time?

How did Carol Singing start?

The word "Carol" means a song of joy. Singing of carols occurred in Europe thousands of years ago, but these were not Christmas Carols. They were Winter Solstice celebrations (December 22nd) as people danced round stone circles such as Stonehenge.

Early Christians took over the pagan solstice celebrations for Christmas using Christian songs. In AD 129, a Roman Bishop said that a song called "Angel's Hymn" should be sung at a Christmas service in Rome, and this was probably the first true Christmas carol.

In the Victorian era many new carols were written and the tradition of walking the streets of London singing carols became very popular.

Try a Fruity Crossword

Across

2. Pudding and jam

5. One sounds like two

6. Man in the moon

8. Odd one with a couple

Down

1. One a day keeps the doc away

3. Sadness without cauliflower

4. After green before red

7. Cannon ammo

A young woman was walking down Oxford Street, wondering what to wear for a Christmas party. Her attention was drawn to a display in one of the shops. Hurrying inside, she asked the salesperson, "May I try on that dress in the window, please?" "Certainly not!" was the frosty reply. "You will use the fitting room, like everyone else."

Lovely Lyric

Somewhere in the middle of all this, Mary found time to write a song. It's deeply passionate, expressing her feelings about being the mother of the child who would put things right in the world. Mary sang it in Aramaic and not in English:

> ***My mind's all stirred up about how great God is,***
> ***And I'm so happy that God is the one who cares about us.***
> ***He's actually noticed a small fry like me.***
> ***Everyone's going to talk about me for years to come,***
> ***For the Powerful One has done amazing things for me.***
> ***No other person is quite like him.***
> ***He loves all people who accept him - right through history.***
> ***He has done some fantastic things,***
> ***But the snobby people he's often pulled down a peg.***
> ***He makes the high-and-mighty feel small,***
> ***But pats the humble folk on the back.***
> ***He feeds hungry people – but the over-fed he ignores.***
> ***Israel is his special interest, right back to Abraham,***
> ***And he's told us so - many times.***

How much of the story on the previous pages can you remember? Try this crossword!

Across

4. A slimy king
5. Worked with wood
6. Foreign visitors
8. Destination

Down

1. Makeshift crib
2. Mode of transport
3. Hillside watchers
7. What the government wanted

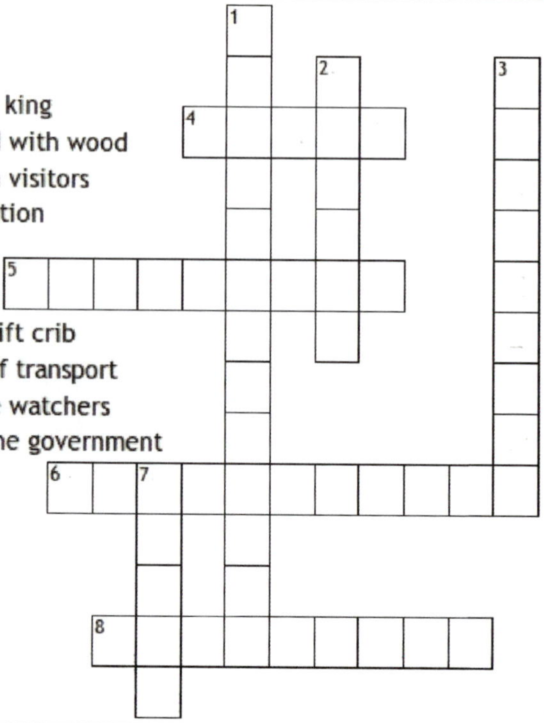

Have your own Grand Slam!

Hidden in this wordsearch are the names of twelve tennis players who have carried off the Grand Slam cups.

(Words in all directions including diagonals)

M	R	E	D	E	N	B	E	C	K	E	R	I	R
B	K	E	I	R	G	D	L	E	R	T	A	D	R
S	A	M	P	R	A	S	O	K	I	N	G	E	S
E	E	I	A	A	F	R	J	N	A	D	A	L	R
I	D	E	E	R	N	C	I	V	O	K	O	J	D
E	R	I	M	E	B	S	T	R	E	V	E	A	N
W	R	E	C	D	S	M	N	L	M	P	R	R	Y
S	E	M	A	E	R	A	A	K	A	R	E	E	R
F	F	F	D	F	Y	I	K	I	R	F	P	A	O
E	A	E	I	E	R	L	E	S	R	C	L	R	A
E	B	R	A	V	R	L	O	R	J	E	G	F	S
R	D	E	G	E	E	I	R	M	U	R	R	A	Y
A	R	R	R	T	P	W	N	E	R	R	A	V	R
A	G	I	P	E	F	E	D	M	I	M	D	C	E

Yet more Christmas riddles
(to make you groan)

What are people who are afraid of Father Christmas called?

What do you get when you cross an apple with a Christmas tree?

Why does Santa Claus have three gardens?

Knock, knock!
Who's there? Snow.
Snow who?
Snow use, I can't remember my name!

Remember that you can find the answers to all the puzzles and riddles at: www.colliercreations.weebly.com

Ninth Day

Geriatric Reward

Joseph and Mary stayed on in Bethlehem to allow the child to grow a bit, and for his mother to recover from the ordeal of the journey and birth trauma. After six weeks they travelled to Jerusalem itself to present the baby to God in the great temple. As they entered the impressive white-marbled courtyards, an old man came up to them with tears in his eyes.

"My name's Simeon," he explained, "and I've worshipped God for many years. I've been looking forward to the time when God would come himself in the form of a man – the one we call 'The Messiah' or 'The Christ'."

Somehow God had tipped him off that if he hung around the temple at this time, then he would see the Messiah for himself. Great was his astonishment and joy when he realised that Mary was carrying this unique baby right before his eyes.

He took the child in his arms and thanked God that he had been privileged to witness what had been promised centuries before. "I'm now ready to finish my life on earth – I've seen the person who will bring light to the whole world."

Thinking Series-ly

See if you can fill in the blank items in the following series...

1. 1, 2, 3, 5, ..., 11, 13
2. Atlanta, Sydney, Athens, ..., London, Rio de Janeiro
3. Chelsea, ..., Arsenal, Arsenal, Man U, Arsenal, Chelsea
4. A, E, F, H, I, ..., L, M, N, T
5. Victoria, Edward, George, ..., George, Elizabeth
6. A, ..., I, O, U
7. 1884, 1888, 1892, 1896, ..., 1908, 1912, 1916
8. John Waite, Frances Quinn, ..., Nadiya Hussain, Candice Brown, Sophie Faldo
9. Red, Orange, ..., Green, Blue, Indigo, Violet
10. "Only Teardrops", "Rise like a phoenix", "Heroes", "..............", "Amar pelos dois", "Toy"

What do Mince Pies signify?

Mince Pies were originally filled with meat, such as lamb, rather than the mix of dried fruits and spices we have today. They were also first made in an oval shape to represent the feeding box that Jesus slept in as a baby, with the top representing his swaddling clothes. In early times they were much larger than today, and often one would suffice as the main course of a meal.

During the Stuart and Georgian times mince pies were a status symbol at Christmas. Very rich people liked to show off at their parties by having pies made in different shapes such as stars, crescents, hearts and flowers. Having pies like this meant one was rich and could afford to employ the best pastry cooks.

Another Sudoku

This one may be a bit trickier than the last one.

Same as before, put numbers in the blank spaces, so that no numbers appear twice in the same row, same column or same 3x3 square region.

	2	9			6		8	7
		7	1		8	4		3
	8	3	5		9	2		6
2		4		9		7	6	
			7	8	1	3	4	
	7		2		4		5	1
7							3	9
9		2	6	1	3	8	7	
		6	9			1	2	5

This is a Transposition Code

The letters of the alphabet are changed according to the grid here, with the upper row being the original letter and the lower being the coded letter.

A	B	C	D	E	F	G	H	I	J	K	L	M
E	V	C	P	R	H	M	A	X	G	U	O	Z
N	O	P	Q	R	S	T	U	V	W	X	Y	Z
K	D	T	Y	I	W	J	S	B	Q	L	N	F

Now try to decode the sentence below back to the original...

EJ CAIXWJZEW NDS CEK ZEUR TRDTOR HDIMRJ JAR TEWJ QXJA JAR TIRWRKJ

Tenth Day

Night Flight

King Herod already had an atrocious track record for killing. It didn't do to lose your head with him, or you might really lose it! Despite his calm demeanour before the visiting astronomers, he was very angry afterwards - and somewhat fearful.

"Another king in my country. I want no more rebellions here," he stormed. "There's only one king here, and that's me! I'm not called Herod the Great for nothing."

When his ire had cooled a trifle, he began to plan action against this possible upstart in Bethlehem. It was obvious the stargazers from the east were not going to come back with information about the child, and so after some months he decided on an inhumane solution to his problem.

"Call the sergeant at arms," he ordered.

Addressing this soldier he commanded him to go to Bethlehem and kill all children under two years old. Reluctantly the officer obeyed, and there was much weeping and screaming in the small village as the murderous edict was carried out.

You might think that's the end of the story – since Jesus was still under two. But God intervened here, and whispered to Joseph to pack up quickly and run away. Nobody was happy about another journey so soon, least of all the donkey. But they managed to escape before the soldiers arrived, and took another long journey to Egypt, beyond Herod's control.

Phonetic Pictures

These pictures all represent the sounds of words from the above story. For example, this one shows holly and a day, meaning "holiday".

It's not in the story, but all the others are! Can you find them?

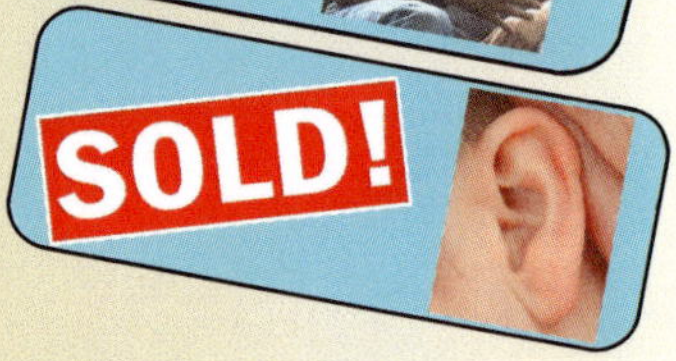

The judge asked the man in the dock, "What are you charged with?"
"Doing my Christmas shopping early," the man replied.
"That's not a crime," the judge said. "When did you do it?"
"Before the shop opened."

Did you get it? (from Sixth Day)

This is a well-known optical illusion that is related to the way in which our brains process information coming from our eyes. Instinctively we think that all chess boards have black and white squares, even when the shadow passes over a square. In fact the shadow on B has been adjusted to be the same colour as square A. But our minds won't accept it.

To try and convince yourself, look at the two vertical bars on the second picture. Are the bars the same colour all over? Yes. Can you see any change of colour where the bars overlap squares A and B? No. Then A and B are the same colour! Agree?

Junior Sudoku

Find numbers (between 1 and 4) to fill all the empty spaces, so that no number appears twice in any row, column or square section.

1	4		2
2			4

Remember that you can find the answers to all the puzzles and riddles at: www.colliercreations.weebly.com

Eleventh Day

Homeward Bound

The refugee family settled into Egypt, where Joseph no doubt found employment for his carpentry skills. After a couple of years the news reached them that King Herod had died.

At that point it seemed safe for the couple with their toddler to return to Israel. Although their home was at Nazareth in the far north of the country, Joseph planned to travel through Bethlehem so that the relatives could see Jesus.

However, as they entered the country they heard that Herod's son, Archelaus, was ruling the land.

Joseph asked one of the local people about this king. "What's this new man like?"

"If you ask me, he's a chip off the old block," was the angry reply. "You'd be best to steer well clear of him."

So they changed their route and headed up the west coast to the home that had been waiting for them for so long.

Jesus grew in the loving atmosphere of the family, and his mother, Mary, knew in her heart that he was the special person that God had promised.

How many edges?

Egypt is famous for its pyramids, and Joseph and his family may have seen these ones. Each pyramid has four sloping edges. How many of these edges can you see in the picture (including the ruined pyramids)?

Check-Mate in Two

You are white, and are playing from the nearer end of the board.

It's your move. Can you check-mate in two moves regardless of how black moves?

Know Your Films

Across

2. Unbelievable (11)
5. Barely possible (10)
7. Very cold (6)
8. Solo sojourn (4-5)
9. Birth story (8)

Down

1. Lamp holder (7)
3. Joyous tootsies (5-4)
4. Universal conflicts (4-4)
6. Feline monarch (4-4)

Why Christmas Puddings?

Christmas (or Plum) Pudding is the traditional end to the British Christmas dinner. But what we think of as Christmas Pudding, is not what it was originally like!

It began as a 14th century porridge called 'frumenty' that was made of beef and mutton with raisins, currants, prunes, wines and spices. This was often more like soup and was eaten as a fasting meal in preparation for the Christmas festivities.

By 1600, frumenty was slowly changing into a plum pudding, having been thickened with eggs, breadcrumbs, dried fruit and given more flavour with the addition of beer and spirits. It became the customary Christmas dessert in the seventeenth century, and remains so in many homes today.

Twelfth Day

Youthful Spirit

Every year during the boyhood of Jesus the family would make the journey back to the region near Bethlehem. Partly it was to keep contact with their extended family, but also to attend the great Passover festival in Jerusalem.

When Jesus was twelve he travelled with his parents from Nazareth in a large contingent of their neighbours and friends. At the end of the week they all set off to return home in one large, noisy group.

At the first night's stop Joseph was filled with consternation! Jesus could not be found among the travellers! He and Mary retraced their steps during the night, and arrived back in Jerusalem just at dawn. After searching likely places, they tried the temple. To their great surprise they found their son sitting in animated discussion with some of the religious boffins.

"Why have you done this to us?" Joseph asked angrily. "We were worried stiff about you."

Jesus showed surprise at this. "Didn't you think I'd be safe in my Heavenly Father's house?"

Then he returned with them to Nazareth, and he grew up to be the special person that the world had long expected.

That's not the end of the story, by a long way - and it's all in the book that we call the Bible.

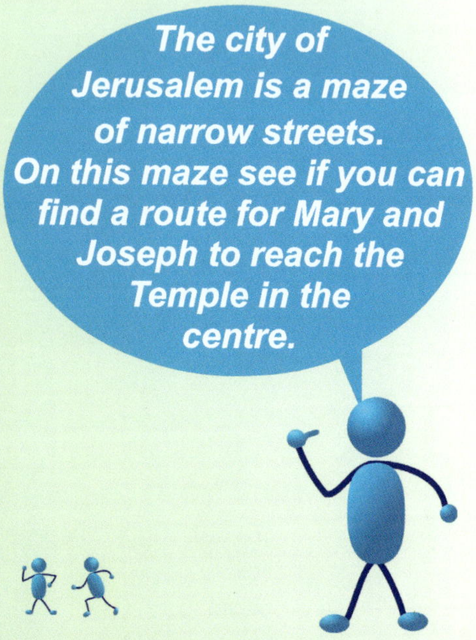

The city of Jerusalem is a maze of narrow streets. On this maze see if you can find a route for Mary and Joseph to reach the Temple in the centre.

Link-Up

Below are some of the places and people from the last twelve days. Try to draw lines linking the items in the two columns...

Jesus's father	Simeon
Jewish king	Jerusalem
Israel's capital	Egypt
Joseph's home	Carpenter
Government action	Joseph
Jesus's refuge	Mary
Foreign visitors	Astronomers
Joseph's job	Herod
Songwriter	Nazareth
Old man	Registration

Learning the Binary Code

This is more than just a fun code! All our computers, phones, and tablets use this. Each letter has a unique binary number.

A=01000001	B=01000010	C=01000011	D=01000100	E=01000101
F=01000110	G=01000111	H=01001000	I=01001001	J=01001010
K=01001011	L=01001100	M=01001101	N=01001110	O=01001111
P=01010000	Q=01010001	R=01010010	S=01010011	T=01010100
U=01010101	V=01010110	W=01010111	X=01011000	Y=01011001
		Z=01011010		

Now try to decode the sentence below...

01001001 01010111 01001001 010110011 01001110 01001111
01010100 01010100 01001000 01000101 01011001 01000101
01001001 01001110 01011001 01001111 01010101 01010010
01001100 01001001 01000110 01010100 01001000 01000001
01010100 01000011 01001111 01010101 01001110 01010100
01001001 01010100 01001001 01010011 01010100 01001000
01001100 01001001 01000110 01000101 01001001 01001110
01011001 01001111 01010101 01010010 01011001 01000101
01000001 01010010 01010011

Christmas is a season not only of rejoicing, but of reflection.
(Winston Churchill)

We are better throughout the year for having, in spirit, become children again at Christmas. *(Laura Ingalls Wilder)*

Unless we make Christmas an occasion to share our blessings, all the snow in Alaska won't make it 'white'. *(Bing Crosby)*

12545146R00015

Printed in Great Britain
by Amazon